Dead Wendy

Richard Carr

FUTURECYCLE PRESS

Mineral Bluff, Georgia

Published by FutureCycle Press
Mineral Bluff, Georgia, USA

ISBN 978-1-938853-00-5

Contents

PART THREE

The Old Man Steps Forward

Acknowledgment

PART ONE

The Boy's Version

I

There are no nurses here—no pills, no machines.
The sickbed is all the comfort you will get,
useless as kind words: sleep well... sweet dreams...
For like the goldfish in the dark pond outside,
a thought moves clearly in your mind:
I must not sleep. I must remain cold.

You watch the faces of tongueless visitors
swim past each other among floating coffee cups.
One might surprise you—it's been so long—
if our old friend can climb the stairs.
You look toward him
as you look toward death.

But love, you start to say, *is just as helpful as...*
or unreal as... These cold nights. No one visits
at midnight, or three, or at liquid dawn. *Unreal...*
You close your eyes to think, always thinking,
and fall asleep. You smile in your sleep, and ask for water.
And I know you, Wendy—I know you are drowning.

II

I can speak with the dead, subterranean Wendy,
just as I can talk to dirt and wood
in their own farfetched dialects.
Here are your bones, under the elm's massive roots.
I brush away the soil and bark
and squeeze the skull by the cheeks.

Murmuring in a fever of decay,
you must give me your last words again.
Whatever doesn't form a scar, I forget.
Your eyes were blue. Or if not blue, then mirrors
and dazzling like a whirlwind of pigeons by the fountain—
a tiny, furious scene… Let me cool your forehead.

I'll visit again in the morning
after the rain soaks through to you, curled in your lair,
and the grackles rise from the lawn,
singing their rough song.
Are you listening?
I love you. I don't know you anymore.

III

The lilacs bloomed that May in continuous rain.
Limping under his black umbrella, the old man
pried at us with his eyes.
Time and age pried at us—but could not divide us
as we strolled by the mere in the park,
our magnificent smiles turned inward.

You had a plan, inexplicable Wendy.
At the last moment you would fill up life with riches,
mahogany and gold, yes, but also wild shrubs and unstoppable rain,
and in blossoming fulfillment of the dream
we traveled to England, your strange ancestral homeland,
to face death—or cure it—with civility and tea.

The estate was grand. But the palace was odious.
The drugs were killers, the clinic a front
for a hospice infested with foregone conclusions.
We woke behind heavy curtains,
and as we drew them open, time rolled forward like thunder,
and we knew you had to die.

IV

We'll go slowly. By jet
the transatlantic flight is too long for talk
but deep enough for tears,
if you want. Put your head on my shoulder.
Just this last difficult sleep
separates the garden of England

from tomorrow. From the doctor
we learned only how to take blood.
He doodled on a pad and said
obey. One word might have been love.
But I was looking at it upside down.
We had better go slowly.

We reach the pinewoods, in due time,
and you row to the old man's cabin across the lake.
Crossing over, night heron, your clear dusk voice
reaches me from the far shore
long after you've stopped waving
and gone indoors.

V

In the old photo, you have almost faded away
against the background of flowering plums.
Everyone is smiling. There used to be occasion
for celebration in the linked arms of friends.
Our banner is still legible,
our protest happy and dire.

Those friends have grown up now, and some have soured
and forgotten how to love the world, and save it.
Stylish, corporate, intellectual, funny,
the jingles they compose slash the price on everything—
shoes, beer, sex—the price of fire driven down
to the price of a match. Passion is cheap.

But it was always free.
That night you and I returned to the plum trees.
I was proud, daring, arrogant in love.
Wearing only white blossoms,
camouflaged in the grove, you were invisible to all
but an owl, calling in a tremulous voice.

VI

I'll give you my barn, dead Wendy,
if it will win you back.
But look! The owl is here—the hooked beak, the ghost face.
Our love is no more than a mouse now, exposed on a hay bale,
and who has the courage anymore
or the hatred to taunt death?

Wendy first-love, I give you all my cows,
for it is their rutted path I follow—
straight through the twisted barn, into the orchard, and up
to the stone markers on the hilltop in the wind.
Follow the cows, and I will meet you among them
in the high grassland of our first days.

In the end I offer you my blackened faith.
Uncouth crows take up arms against sorrows
that I enfold in my wings. One corn kernel replanted,
and the whole hailed-out crop comes back to life
—though we will not harvest.
Magnanimous Wendy, we are spirits of the green prairie.

VII

Our story began classically, once upon a time,
and quickly therefore the fairytale turned gruesome.
I walked out of the magical forest one night
and promptly grew up. I took an interest in killing-machines
and began recording their exploits in combat. Luckily,
the wars ended—although the deaths kept coming.

For too many years I read only ironclad books,
cutting off new beginnings, never to be a child again
and say forever-and-ever, and believe it,
while you kissed gods, held lightning in your hands,
flew over every sea and chimney on the globe
on your deathbed blanket.

Returning to the forested stories of our youth,
hoping we might stay in love forever
and ever after live backwards happily,
I go to your books, high on a dusty shelf,
but find they have grown quiet, drowsy,
like the spiders. They are content.

VIII

All right woman, where did you hide the keys?
Where did you put your tears, the can opener?
Where are the clean bedsheets?
Where in the hell is England? Where?
Death, shit, rats! Woman, where
is my collection of grotesques?

I can't live with you anymore.
Get out of my house.
Don't call me.
I don't need your beauty. Cut your hair.
Damn your brains.
This is my final offer.

All right woman. Just leave me the checkbook.
Just leave me the pictures, the mirror,
and the armchair. We sat together in the big chair,
didn't we. Didn't we make plans?
Who will help me if you leave?
Just help me find my keys—and I'll let you go.

IX

The embodiment of everything opposite, I stand
cock up at the plywood bar, a pitcher of cold beer
cascading down the marble staircase of my throat.
I know the great man's belch, the cheering crowd,
and also the nadirs and nemeses,
the smoking butt of life, the precarious ash.

Once a lover of auld lang syne, antithetical Wendy,
it's death now. Like you, I've written a hundred last testaments:
This is what I am when I am nothing.
Already half dead to everyone I've loved or tried to love,
I bequeath to the half-living my remaining worldly beliefs—
a rabble of starlings feeding noisily.

With nothing left to give or be, let's devote our lives
to sex gods, pasta, grass, jazz, bliss.
Let us glorify ennui in the neon lounge, late nights,
our sequined vagrancy and the black-tie moon.
At last call, we'll howl with lunar intelligence.
Loose dogs on the street, we'll sleep in the dirt.

X

I drink rain. The old man fumbled for his umbrella
and took furtive shelter from your love. Though he still drinks
straight whiskey soberly, he is clearly disconcerted
by the algae on my lips and says he'll quit tomorrow
when he is a peat bog, tomorrow when he is oil, coal, diamond—
tomorrow when he's worthless. Better to drink

rain. The teeth-mother and sky-father poured their blood
into sacrificial goblets, it is said, to consecrate
the marriage of our progenitors, mythic children
who in their turn gulped from blood-tainted rivers and ran wild
celebrating each other, the deaths they would conceive,
and the end of their terrible nakedness on Earth. Naturally I

drink rain. Drink rain, all, to primordial Wendy
for whom time was a dark and thunderous sea
and she awash on the shores of consciousness
until the days became cities and the nights became winters
and she lost all our names in the drunken surge.
Drink rain. You stones and green seedlings, drink rain.

XI

In the hierarchies of angels, heavenly Wendy,
catastrophe split the world in two, the happy families
hauling off their jade pools and beds of dark ruby,
the rebellious band all things bastard and broken.
I wanted to be a man of principles, to stand in the middle,
as the wars burned forests, infants, and devils together.

The old man carved in ivory his intricate headaches
and displayed them in his winter palace
with his paintings of victors.
You lived in the trailer park with your beat-up Chevys,
your painted wings peeling, your plates and cribs
a waste of time.

The nectar of my flowers was gasoline,
and I loved the fresh atoms of detonation,
loved the cataclysms of governments falling,
the thrown bricks—loved reporting the story.
I loved my amorality, hellish Wendy,
having nothing else to love.

XII

The old man lives out all his fantasies,
including his worst nightmares,
drearily. His plots weave:
"Like the castles of winter
recalled in the spring country,"
the beginning follows the end.

There is no reason to believe he will die
like you. He has no expiration date.
His youth needs no ironing.
The old rat in fact likes the rain.
He endures by force of will
—eighty years, ninety…

It is a half-hearted longevity,
methodical. He counts the apple blossoms,
the untold millions in the grove,
but has forgotten the one petal that fell in your lap.
He is an old root, Wendy.
You should live instead.

XIII

We started as neighbors, and you promised
to bring me tomatoes from your garden.
But how could you? Your only produce—
marble columns and tidy hedges—
could never fit in my efficiency refrigerator.
I am a small man—a dime friend, a nickel bag.

I have a recurring dream of leaking quills,
our lives blotted out.
In the treetop, the crow and owl are lovers,
stabbing each other.
Maybe we deserve each other. If only
for these brutal moments.

There is a stone wall dividing our yards.
You hang your arms over. I chat
smiles. I'll miss your flowering crabapple.
You generalize. You'll miss blossoming May.
You hold a packet of oregano seeds.
I finger my keys.

XIV

The grackle wading in the wet grass says
there will always be a lawn here for you,
maple leaf, if you should ever choose to fall.
You consider the offer—turning red, gold—
then laugh and fly among the twigs.
You don't take gravity very seriously.

But I do. Up to my knees in concrete,
I have all the necessities and cogwheels of life
at my disposal, my hands just two of many
precision instruments. I live among machines,
green Wendy. Gloomy and meticulous,
I reconstruct their tumbled and forgotten dreams.

Have I gotten it all wrong: hierarchies, antitheses?
You must teach me how to whirl in the wildwood,
and I will chase you through the spring evening
to the pagan dance. In a clearing shivering with dew,
you will transcend the moon-thin air, willow spirit,
and descend into my heavy arms.

XV

Trees fighting the great thunderheads,
tall cottonwoods swaying at the breaking point,
we seethe in each other's arms.
We crash against each other heedlessly,
howling in the sky, in the wind and flying debris,
until our strength is exhausted in the storm.

In the downpour below, silent time slows.
A car skids off the road, windshield
shattering, the bodies ejecting—
no time left for them
to make promises. They can go no further.
Steady rain continues through the night.

High above the clouds, the moon slows in its path.
It will become famous for its blindness
and decrepitude. It will lack the will to lift the tide.
Ships will still come and go,
but the captains will get no sleep
on the tranquil sea.

XVI

This is the end, Wendy, my monkey,
my goat. My rampages no longer insurable,
I'm forced to think covertly.
The other baboons squatting at the bar
suspect me of foul play—but say nothing
and slide their eyes neatly back into place.

It's a quiet night at the watering hole.
Nothing has hit the fan.
A woman too gray for the crowd
swivels on her stool and yawns.
Her boyfriend only looks like an actor.
His deadpan perfectly expresses his ambition.

I stare unfashionably into my glass of beer,
searching the unseeable deeps.
I've developed a nervous tic, a lewd wink,
and a seasick thirst for immortality.
But I can't sit here alone, mouthing words.
I'm outmoded. I should go.

XVII

It's over. Thunder, heroics, love.
And in the sky—no sign of anything.
We wait. It is the end of spring,
the end of rain, the end
of green and energetic life,
and the blue that pierced the sky

must fade. We linger. Summer passes,
consuming everything in its path,
the lilacs burnt and crumbling,
the pasture bitten all the way down.
On the gravel road lies a dead cat, its open gut
disgorging to the harrowed plains

the lives it held. Time comes. Autumn almost over,
the cornfields darken, Wendy my crow,
then blaze to yellow for the harvest, the tall stalks falling
into the restless sleep of change. One life
creates another. It is a process
of decay. Early snow. Black wings.

XVIII

Your mourners walk daintily in the slush.
They enter the wake in soaked shoes, fresh grief quivering
wildly up their legs. Memories rush at them like birds
crashing against the living room window.
Everyone hugs. Except you.
Your body is empty.

It is wrong of you to be so quiet.
While we jitter in delirious ekstasis,
you shrink inside your dress.
The dress reminds me of the little cabbage moths
—yellow ones, white ones—
twitching in your kitchen garden.

I smell your hair again,
aroused by the fragrance
of the tiny lily of the valley.
I feel your kiss on my neck,
warm, wanting. You ask me in a whisper
to come home with you.

XIX

Throw open the kitchen window and breathe!
We'll have lilacs all May, and then mown hay,
and every time I butter your toast
we'll live six more months in love.
Let our mornings last forever!
Only—let me make new endings forever.

You never gave birth to a child.
I will be your child—a cherub, I promise.
You didn't want to return from England.
I will go there, bringing more rain.
You never married the one you loved.
I will see to his needs. He's old now.

I built my house in the old man's woods.
I had a dream there of breaking through ice on the river,
skeleton Wendy, and reaching up to clasp your hand.
I saw the cold, familiar light blazing in your eye sockets,
but I was a lover of darkness,
and withdrew, slipping beneath the surface.

XX

The flower I bring is engineered,
flown over the Atlantic like a cadaver in refrigeration,
and delivered into my hands.
It was once a living thing.
Now it is reduced to a formation of ice crystals, in the shape of a tulip,
and coloring agents: blue with flecks of gold.

The construct symbolizes my love,
our fidelity to a lost friend,
and the richness of her love in return.
I don't know how else to pray.
My soul moves with glacial slowness,
but it carries this last bloom.

A mountaineer who perished on a high slope,
Wendy lies half buried in a drift: frozen, stopped,
with frost-ferns on her eyes, icy teeth,
and that blue turn of lips we know.
Brush away the snow. We'll set our brittle flower—
gently, old man—upon her silver cheek.

Richard Carr § 29

PART TWO

Dead Wendy Responds

Richard Carr § 31

I

I thought the underworld was a silent one
until your shouting shook the trees
and the black raindrops rolled off the black leaves,
splashed on the lawn of long night,
and seeping down through the dark soil
trickled across my flesh like acid.

So much trembling and commotion
I have not seen since life. There I was oak,
but you were fire and saw through to the molecules of me.
Even now I am afraid of your voice,
you sleepless monster, you storm whirling at my bedside.
The sickbed, the grave-bed—the terror never ends.

Yet there were safe moments, quiet minutes
folded cat-snug against your chest. That embrace,
recalled through all the minutes of the years intervening,
has remained to me, in my little bunk, a comfort.
Then you—storm-fire, lily fool—you kissed the dead.
And my lips opened for you.

II

You brought flowers, lilacs. Thank you.
Now take them back.
I have no desire for spring perfumes.
I am not hungry. I do not yearn.
I cannot feel my perfect toes, so far away.
I cannot see your face.

Under the cool sun of the shadow world,
you are a boiling fog.
Obsessed with breathing, you pander to the living
with your dulcimer love.
You must fold your hands and back away looking down.
You are no longer my valiant.

What could you know about the hard earth
and our needs?
You bring handfuls of dirt,
but we spit it out.
We of the tombs and pits and anonymous trenches—
we have no love for your kind.

III

Leave the damned farm.
The tractor won't start. The corn won't grow.
The pigeons moaning in the haylcft
rain down shit on your shoulders
as you prepare the noose.
You should leave the farm soon.

You're right: without your bright corn kernels,
the crows abandon the dry fields
and scrap for rations of the dead cat's coiled guts.
The cat last dined on the dusty pelt of a starved mouse,
her mouth still clogged with dust.
It's a hard drought—but not your undoing.

Loosen the rope, and you will understand.
Turn around.
Your look of bewilderment touches me.
I see a poor man—lank hair, torn shirt pocket,
sagging jeans. Chin up.
I'll start the tractor for you.

IV

Meet me in the prodigious city
by the opera house fountain splashing in the bright night.
You must pick the street grit from my dress.
I'll pick street grit from your hair.
Then we'll watch the great soprano and the great tenor die,
slowly, under the great king's heavy tears.

When the time comes, take me back to fire-blackened London.
Rat-blackened, bomb-blackened,
the city that ruled around the globe
still glints ominously.
My city of gardens!
City of dark rooms, remember me.

Leave me at last in Pompeii, sweetly satisfied
with wine and seafood and sun. I am the green and gold mosaic
on the bathhouse wall—a reclining nude, life-size,
with eyes of decadent lapis.
Brush the sand grains from my lashes and leave me there,
unearthed, under the hot blue sky.

V

I wish I were sitting in the big armchair,
the photo album open on my lap,
one hand touching a picture of us at the beach,
the other touching my throat,
a string of pearls around my neck,
a white bedsheet covering my stillness.

I wish for these comforts.
I wish you had buried with me all
your tokens of love—the mirror, the hairbrush
—instead of your grinding desire.
If you could only let me go,
you would not find me so inscrutable.

You would not pound your fist.
You would not scream at me.
You would not try to possess me.
You would not seize me in your arms—
and I would not sicken you
with the exhaust of my breath.

VI

You disguise your softness with a beard.
Pretending to grow old,
you feign deafness in one ear,
complain about cold rooms,
cry easily.
Bastard! You forgot the color of my eyes.

But the grass stains on your knees
show your age. Blowing toy trumpets,
your tin armies march across my grave
in obedience to your childish imperatives,
your dire make-believe devotion
all bluster and snot.

Look at the fox pups creeping from the den.
Blinking, unperplexed, they shake their tufted ears
and dive into a rough game of tag.
You are better off with them
and the honest, toothsome youthfulness
that I first loved. For I love their danger.

VII

You have been a poor student of death.
But learn:
Death is not like sleep. It is not forgetfulness, oblivion,
or nothingness.
Death is not decomposing flesh and skeletal remains,
not dirt.

Death is a long warehouse full of daisies
and kicked buckets.
Death is swimming with the fishes,
which you'd enjoy.
Death is a pale horse waiting for me in the meadow,
his neck bending exquisitely.

A rabbit in the claws of the cat—
that is life.
The brick wall spray-painted with the riots of our hearts—
that is life.
The silence that you bring to my grave
is life.

VIII

Sober, you were useless to me. Drunk,
you danced beautifully, your hands rising
and turning like two tethered birds.
My belly was a green mountain,
and yours was a cloud passing over,
a thunderhead of dark yearning.

A yellow pencil in your teeth,
chewed at jet speed, you crossed the Pacific
to photograph combat, orchids,
and refugees crouched by their small, smoky fires.
Sober, you were despicable, a licensed harbinger.
While you lit cigarettes, people died.

After the war you followed rock bands
until each one was destroyed. Somehow
you knew where their airplanes would crash.
You trailed the coroner to hotel rooms. You heard gunshots
outside nightclubs. You watched the dancing stop, each time,
and start over more wildly.

IX

I never understood your drinking habit,
your gin martini so refined, like your white cuffs,
and yet so lewd, served to you by half-dressed girls
blinking in and out of existence
in the strobe lights and smoke of a thumping disco.
What were you looking for in that mindless night?

I had made you a steak, gory rare, and placed red
tulips in a vase. Late, when you banged through the apartment door,
I was in bed, still awake—so hating
you and wanting you that I couldn't move.
My owl eyes saw everything
and nothing in the darkness.

That morning I would find tulip petals
scattered in the bathroom like blood
splashed on the sink, in the toilet, on the black tile floor.
In the night I'd heard you walking from room to room—heard
the door again—heard your voice *Taxi!* down on the street *Taxi!*
—then only street noise honking and hammering as the sun rose.

X

I'll grow tomatoes for you.
We'll move to the country.
You'll drive your old pickup truck
slowly down the dirt road home,
and I'll have what I want,
a diet of quiet loaves.

You are my sunflower, always bending
toward me—but also drawn terribly
into earthly conflagrations:
civilizations perishing in the deserts,
orgasms of imperial power in the free markets,
the victims and assassins taking turns on the talk shows.

I prefer the farmer's honest wit.
I will have you.
Like the blue butterfly fluttering
in my cupped hands,
I will have you, voiceless.
I will feed you.

XI

I am burned and stoned and I can moralize
through migraine heroin thorazine.
I hate your intervention
and the busy signal on the red phone
and the cattle falling out of my ears,
their imperatives you and your limp smile.

My jaw hurts talking to you.
I make conversation, always cheerful,
while you feed on me.
A ghoul from the start,
you leaned into my open coffin
and your breath stank of old loves.

I can't live like this anymore.
Get out.
Grow up. Get a job.
Cut your hair. Use your head. Live!
You have the promise of granite blocks, the fate of marble columns.
Build your own mansion, mausoleum, theater.

XII

I suppose I'll miss you.
Who else will butter my toast?
You called me a maple leaf,
a being of the golden breeze.
Who else could see that?
Who would promise so much?

Thank you for staying young for me—
thank you for that rainfall.
And thank you for giving up your chair to the old man.
I loved him too. Now he's dying.
He has a new house and a new dog
and a new pain in his gut—another surgery.

I suppose we share that fear,
the certainty of decay,
the breaking of all relationships.
When he limps home early from the tavern,
with excuses and watery eyes,
thank you for following him. He still misses me.

XIII

I remember the long lawn flowing
like a river rushing down from the manor house
to a pool of white sheep.
Peacocks flying up the hill
are received by yellow trees that bow
and lift the exhausted birds.

Inside the mansion, in a private chamber full of mist,
I try to sleep.
There are no family portraits to watch over me,
no tapestries to tell me stories, no furniture
except my steel sickbed piled with blankets.
I try to review my life.

I wonder if anyone can hear me.
How can a voice penetrate this fog?
These are not the usual shrouds of England.
Sometimes I hear a screech in a far room.
Some nights devils come silently to wake me
and enfold me in their dark wings.

XIV

You carry pictures of yourself in your wallet,
your measurements.
Your eyes reflect the flash
of gunfire on television.
You are the whimper
of a generation that howled.

Who else will you kiss?
You gave me plums,
dark, ready,
fermenting in their own skins—
your chocolate smile
dripping.

You wove of twigs a peace symbol
when I said your talk galls me.
In answer,
naked, grinding against tree bark,
I thought to myself, and kept to myself.
Who else will you kiss?

XV

The dead observe our lovemaking
with the icy fondness of their kind,
longing for the shadows we conceive
that these may rise to the highlands
where only silent starlight shines
on grass blades weary of color.

In the sprawling gloom of the city below,
the factories of nothingness leak black smoke.
Your voice is the smell of a public toilet.
Always sniffing, I insist we remain hairless.
Our apartment is a cube in a stack of cubes.
We are always touching something.

Waking to snowfall in a wilderness,
we slap our gloved hands together
and puff the cold air.
The wintering geese refuse to lift their wings
but stand aloof on the banks of a slow river
hot with our runoff.

XVI

I was your B-movie gypsy,
a fortune-teller with a shrewd eye
for love and gold. I saw a tornado blossoming,
white lilacs whipping in the wind, purple ones
beating the earth. It was our passion
destroying everything we owned.

We moved into separate lives.
I had my collection of paper snowflakes
and lake agates, the old man,
and a modest death. I relaxed then,
at ease through all the years alone,
in my bed of silks and simple pine.

By the time you accepted my death,
my love for you, like my flesh,
had diminished.
But I spoke to you, and in your exuberance
you lifted me from the grave
in a swirl of rainbow dresses.

XVII

For his cracked teeth,
give him soft bread and brie.
For the tremors in his spotty fingers,
give him caviar and cigars on a silver tray.
He was the one I loved.
He deserves your luxuries.

For his glances, that I miss, his eyes clouding,
give him angry lakes and pelting rain.
For his hissing, dusty voice,
give him the baritone clarity of thunder receding.
He was the one I loved, while I could.
He deserves good weather.

For his lucid nightmares of crows and falling trees,
give him one bright petal dropped from the apple blossom.
For the silted river of his dark, slow memory,
give him my dresses and perfume.
He was the one I loved, not you.
He deserves our happiness.

XVIII

It's over. Rain, sun, storm—
we embraced each in its time.
But summer turned away from us,
and fall turned against us,
and still we did not move indoors with the crickets.
The garden felt right for mice like us.

Snow fell from beautiful heights,
and burrowing into the drifts
we made our small but intrepid promises.
The owl heard, looked,
lurched from the pine bough,
his great wings sweeping down darkness.

We fled into the night.
Our journeys there made us wary and savage.
Like rats, we ate everything. Our mating
created a death so full of love
it would never leave us.
But we were young. We were never safe.

XIX

I'm cold. I must not sleep.
In the fireplace burn my letters—
sparks rising in startled flocks—
and my last testaments to keep us warm.
Consider yourself lucky today.
I accept your flowers.

Into this winter of muskrat furs
and horse hides and candles melted
to the edge of drowning,
you imported tulips—blue
with flecks of gold. I accept
the stiff gestures of the moon.

This is how we survive. We break apart
the rocking chair and the kitchen table
for fuel. We curl together
as tightly as possible. You live,
and weep, and clutch the blankets.
And I accept it. I must remain cold.

XX

I'll trek with you as far as the river.
Lace up your boots, and close your heavy coat.
Pull on your mittens, leather over wool.
You can cross on the ice.
There will be no parting words between us.
Your legs will tremble in the cold.

You must run to keep up with me
and see my fierce dance in the woods,
the last you will know of me,
for now my dresses are white,
now flurries of snow—
my voice pitched high above the wind.

You are dishonest in the blizzard.
Which way should you turn?
But the river buckles, and you crash through.
You clatter in the loose ice, taking huge gasps,
until your will hardens, and you let go,
close your eyes, and slide under.

PART THREE

The Old Man Steps Forward

I

At the pace of cattle trundling across the clodded pasture,
all relationships will be broken
by nightfall:
the barbwire cut, the barn on fire, the house gutted—
doors unhinged,
suitcases thrown through windows.

We walk away—into the sea, into the air, into the earth—
passing through sunburned youth,
spiraling old age, and premeditated death
in an afternoon.
Through cloudless dusk and moonless night, our cricket voices
chirp ever more faintly.

Each morning, the city's blue glass and golden skyline
springs to its feet: ten million souls
in cubicles, behind doors, in aeries,
and some below, behind dumpsters, in sewers.
Why do we part ways? The plane tree's leaves fall serenely—
and soar up on whistling gusts.

II

Wendy traveled to England for her health
and to live a dream. Or to die in it.
But the hedgerows could not fence out her illness.
The trout stream could not wash away the cancer.
The manor was a dark, infested hospice, the sculpted shrubs
a dreariness. And the peacocks? A complete fiasco.

She came back to my cabin in the woods,
rowing painfully across the lake. I had hopes for her—
hope that my meager health would warm her,
that my kisses might return color to her cheeks,
that the tamarack winds could breathe clean life into her.
But the outhouse was her abode. A lonely emergency room.

Wrapped in white sheets, she would never descend
the great sweeping staircase of her English dream.
I was the thick bone and muscle of the language,
and my words were the naked thew and sinew of my heart.
But I couldn't lift Wendy from the sickbed, couldn't carry her.
Unable to bear her emaciation. A desiccated, black tongue.

III

Damning the ungodly brains of freaks and drunks
who see the blurred world clearly,
I drink my straight whiskey soberly.
Once I flew on forest business for the owls,
carrying their messages on rainy nights.
Now I roost on a mountain ledge, sipping dew.

I have become a Zen master souse. I perceive:
Even the great soaring-birds fly tethered
on mile-long cords. The knot of my crossed legs
likewise fastens me to earth. I cannot fall,
nor can I sleep, for unconsciousness
is a shaky sobriety. A species of homelessness.

Derelict, destitute, the aesthetics of the mass market
grotesque, I drink the infinite—infinite
varieties of beauties. A good shot. A good fuck.
A good man guzzles such songs, belches them
into the valley below. Sheep there nibble white shoots,
breathe the soil's musk. That final perfume.

IV

Wendy was never old
but always a terrible blue flower unfolding.
Patient as a fed cat, quiet as a book,
she waited for my visit. Always late,
I came to her sickbed and found her floating above it,
just a sliver of moon, crying sweetly to herself.

I looked away. And at that moment the boy returned.
The invader marched across the lawn,
trampled the twig and bark shrine of my grief,
broke the locks on the house,
blustered into Wendy's bedroom, and took her
for his own—lifting her, kissing her tears.

That hurt. I felt old. I looked in the mirror,
and the shaved head of death looked back, rotting
slightly. It sang a mad song! I backed away.
I would start over, in the forest, and grow again—
a seed in the mulch, a sapling, an oak of many limbs
—and build a ship to sail beneath the moon.

V

He brought you flowers made of shade.
A shade sitting beside him on the park bench,
you knew when the rain fell—only that—and vanished
for long moments in the shadow of a passing cloud.
He felt alone, dreary in your presence. Somehow
springtime always broke his heart.

I arrived in that season with the first ominous robin,
disguised myself as a tall gentleman
leaning firmly on a cane.
My feet were already deep in the dirt of my long life
by the time you saw my devouring smile
unfolding like a black umbrella.

Glowering Wendy, dour under your dark sun,
I would remain silently aware of you—and of the boy,
whose world made you savage.
For you returned his gifts with brutal kisses,
and his daylight was Hell to you, and his rain—
the catalyst of your blistering spite.

VI

I prayed to peyote crows to give me Wendy—
a greedy supplication to a disdainful conclave.
Blood trickles not from the knees of gods, but from ours only,
so when in the circle of dark firs where the dark ones gather
I asked only for a test of my faith,
the rookery erupted with wild and hateful laughter.

Without the crows' noisy wings and leap into air
but only gray brains,
and eyes not full of purpose and understanding
but stupid tears,
I still managed to follow my guides
into the dream they had prepared for me.

In the morning, lulled from my sleep in the forest canopy,
I turned away from the crows, demure for the moment,
and yet for their strange kindnesses
thanked them, for they brought to me on their black wings
Wendy in her black gown gliding
down the staircase of night.

VII

I foresaw the coming of civilization
and ran in mock terror.
It was scary—but I was alive!
The great wars had ended with the clasping of hands and hugging in the
    streets,
and everyone who could got pregnant.
Then they got jobs and built the suburbs.

Lonesome, I spent a generation hiding out in a jazz club,
rearranging the whiskers on my face every few years.
The wars, meanwhile, got harder and harder,
and people started to complain.
The rearrangement of whiskers was one form of protest,
and I started to write marching songs to accompany my beard.

While the boy wrote war stories for the wires,
with his heroes and joes, mothers and mined pastures,
I composed lullabies for Wendy, little melodies with small notes,
our dim stars burrowing through the night sky,
and soon she came to me, and pressed her forehead against my shoulder,
and we had peace.

VIII

We had peace
beneath the linden trees,
flowering, finely scented,
almost imperceptible,
our kisses dry
like the brushing together of leaves.

We were already ghosts.
On the boulevard of victories,
among the tourists gazing upward,
we stood for an hour in the shade
of a warm day,
our affair—a stillness.

War had reached into us
and made our eyes round and dark,
intent, forgiving of all sins.
We heard the traffic again on the street
and hurried to a room
and closed the door.

IX

The boy confronts me at the seaport, his foul language
in full stride strangling dead horses and regurgitating
mangled cormorants flapping madly at my feet.
I stand forward in the gale of fish breath and spraying spit
until at length the storm calms in him and gradually settles
to beating the piers of my shoulders with ineffectual fists.

We both love her.
We cannot capture and keep her.
She is leaving us.
Gulls cry, rigging clangs—
But we cannot shake hands today.
She's still too near.

Warehouses—modern, monotonous—line the docks across the inlet.
The walls and roofs of thin, metallic gray
reflect no sun and cast no shadow.
But the structures are vast, and they have rights and laws of their own.
If there are people, they are too small to see.
Like me, I think the boy fears walking one day in those storehouses alone.

X

Spiritus Wendy! I offer you the fable of the hedgerow mice
and their leafy garden,
including one aria about produce,
a duet at the kitchen window,
and my promise to meet you there, under the very wings of the hermit
   thrush,
and bring you back alive.

The boy can't even remember the color of your eyes.
Or maybe he loves a color no one else can see.
He looks at you with pupils balanced
on a highwire.
His realism sees you dead.
Who will you choose?

You dote on the corpse that was you,
preening and painting it.
Knowing you will soon be alone
with no one to compete for your attention,
you file the long, long fingernails, nonchalant,
and adjust the shredded remains of your hair.

XI

Pushing dirt down onto you was difficult.
Your silence was hard.
No words for me.
In the language of reversal,
all things are unsaid—
beauties faded, praises retracted.

The boy arrived with a tuft of clover in his hand,
and you shrieked weeping obscenities
as though he had come to hurt you
with his gift.
He did not bear your ferocity well.
I thought I would prefer it.

I returned to the site in every season,
bending closer and closer to the ground
until I finally succumbed
to the scrub and weeds growing without sentience
and awoke—
thin, watery-eyed, and new.

XII

I live in a house grown from acorns.
In the uppermost chamber lie my treasures—
a hoard of ivory, catgut, mother-of-pearl, and mahogany,
all out of reach—my mechanical knees unsafe on the spiral staircase.
In the basement, I strike matches with frostbitten hands.
When I get a candle to light, I sing to it carefully.

The boy's meandering flat wanders like a stream through pastureland.
His books are stacked on rocks and balanced on fence posts.
In his green study he scatters seeds, and when the sparrows sweep through
he is reminded of helicopter gunships
picking off easy targets.
In the morning he takes a cold drink.

Wendy's house is a fairyland castle.
She flies down the halls and through the galleries
on a magic carpet made of fog.
There are milk and cookies in every room, such is her hospitality,
yet she has just two teacups,
and these are preserved in separate secret vaults.

XIII

The boy was never hippie enough for Wendy,
who in one summer went from mush-brained groupie
to brilliant militant in thick glasses and hair dyed black.
He dug her plum-blossom complexion,
I the tart mulberry lips.
And so ours was the infatuation of simpletons.

We could not keep pace with her transformations.
Braless, tall, angry, freakish, wasted,
liberated and terrorized, loved and raped,
the violence of modernity tore her apart
as it lifted her up—
while we popped open cans of beer.

In the end, we were not tough enough
for a dying woman. A drenched cat,
she lashed out at any inconvenience,
bit loved ones, disgorged lobsters of hate
upon all others. And we didn't have the guts
or intelligence to be her friend.

XIV

Wendy is afraid.
I must find a better way of burying her,
a blouse and plain business skirt
too vulnerable, too cold.
She holds a tiny lily of the valley between two fingers—
a very small prayer.

The boy is never afraid.
He raises his head out of the foxhole,
snaps three pictures of incoming fire,
and sinks down.
He jots notes. Wendy crosses his mind,
but he concentrates on the wide-open faces of soldiers.

Wendy is waiting for him.
Their thoughts are alike.
They will walk in a monochrome garden,
admiring its stillness.
There can be no promises made concerning death,
yet all swear love forever.

XV

I abhor the boy's clandestine life—
and desire it. Drinking in solitude
all through the summer afternoon
and under the thundershowers of cool evening,
he crawls home late, wet, sniggering,
and Wendy feeds him.

Wendy's generosity appalls me.
Milkweed, hackberry, and apple blossoms scented
beyond the comprehension of my broken nose,
I do not understand her abundance.
Does she control the weather, move clouds,
turn the rain on and off?

In her autumn—I suspect it is her autumn—
the air is dusty, dry. I chew brown leaves,
hungering dysfunctionally for emptiness.
It comes:
I go to the castle of winter to starve
without Wendy.

XVI

In a roofless house of madness and demons,
I live alone.
In the elms gather the crows of my old intellect,
a terrible, silent politburo sitting in judgment.
At the door, the idiot-savant moon peeks through the keyhole.
A sawdust voice oozes red wine.

The words form a bubble on my lip.
I look up from my book, closing it with slow brutality.
The drugged, blue clouds gurgle their vows—
that lightning will strike, that trees will shatter.
And this old rat will not survive the night
without hurting someone. The scabbed moon first.

The sun rises explosively and rains down its bright radiation.
Eyes bulging out of my head, I glare like a caught fish
at the bloodshot world and the numb stumbling
of its growth: the greenery, the trickery, and their unrepentant
reinvention of life. Spring upon spring, the hatchling
falls from the nest. The blue jay screaks! The eyes glare.

XVII

My dinner is cold.
I stared for an hour at a good T-bone,
thinking of a pasture with a muddy pond.
The baked potato,
wrinkled and spotted like the top of my hand,
reminds me of suppers in a dark kitchen

many years ago.
My legs were never more than cornstalks,
good for sprinting. *So tall! He'll be a star!*
Now they are cold.
I limp because my belly aches.
The surgeries cannot cure me of autumn

or the new snow.
No child ever made an angel in my yard,
gathered lilacs from the hedge. No bee stings.
The house is cold.
I love you, Wendy. I miss the cows.
No one calls me to bed. Yet at last I will go.

XVIII

It's over. The seasons, the pain. Everything passes.
The low clouds. Hopeless afternoon. I am almost late.
Snow has begun to fall.
I have already begun to cry—an old fool.
The twisted elms rasp and sway in the early dusk.
I am late.

The house is quiet. Full of visitors.
Coffee, the only permissible sustenance,
steams in white cups, in nerveless fingers.
Some breathe: *She's already gone.* Some say *no.*
The heavy drapes are drawn aside, the night
a black monument. Few venture upstairs.

Wendy's lips do not move.
She is almost weightless now, like a leaf. She hisses
my name—this is what I wanted!—
and recedes into sleep. A dress rehearsal. No applause.
I listen.
Fat snowflakes splash against the window.

XIX

Slouched up in bed, Wendy accepted embraces from everyone.
Last, I brought her a choral symphony of kisses,
hastily composed. She hummed a little, gazing at me, or through me,
and like the last lonely goldfish in the dark pond outside,
a thought swam slowly in her mind.
Then ice crept across the surface and thickened.

According to plan, Wendy's casket rested on a mound of fake snow
and blue tulips.
The rows of mourners leaned on each other, head on shoulder,
like melting statues.
My stomach caved in like an old barn. My rusty knees crumbled.
Strangers gripped my arms painfully.

At the cemetery, a release of live butterflies
floated down to the frosted ground and died.
Now the strength of Orpheus beat in my chest—but no song.
I stayed until all was sealed, closed, covered.
Alone finally, I sat in the dirt—time booming in my ears.
Stars rose, untroubled, and shivered in the night sky.

XX

One day I saw dead Wendy walking naked in the snow,
gliding through the pines and rising mist.
Her flesh, white and dusty like birch bark, peeled away
and quickly she was gone.
I said good-bye to no one, to the woods—
and shambled into town through slush.

I wanted a last whiskey with the boy.
We sang of the dead together
and competed to make the best goat-song.
Then out on the street, he said goodnight quietly.
Fell to his knees in the snow.
Rose—smiling wanly—and said: *This is difficult.*

Drunk bastard fell through river ice that night.
He took a wrong turn.
I hope he fell all the way through
to the green prairie—that was a better sea!
But I am drowning in the same drunken delusion.
Wendy is impossible now, for ordinary men.

Acknowledgment

Grateful acknowledgment is made to *Many Mountains Moving,* in which these poems first appeared: "The Boy's Version" I through IV.

Other Poetry Collections by Richard Carr

Books

Imperfect Prayers
One Sleeve
Ace
Street Portraits
Honey
Mister Martini

Chapbooks

Butterfly and Nothingness
Letters from North Prospect

*Covert art, "Reflected Light & Flower" by Stephen Candler
(spcandler.zenfolio.com); cover design, interior art treatment (from
"Tulip, fading glory…," by Cecile Graat, gracedesign.nl), and book design
by Diane Kistner (dkistner@futurecycle.org); Adobe Garamond Pro text
with Helvetica Neue titling*

About FutureCycle Press

FutureCycle Press is dedicated to publishing lasting English-language poetry and flash fiction books, chapbooks, and anthologies in both print-on-demand and ebook formats. Founded in 2007 by long-time independent editor/publishers and partners Diane Kistner and Robert S. King, the press incorporated as a nonprofit in 2012. A number of our editors are distinguished poets and authors in their own right, and we have been actively involved in the small press movement going back to the early seventies.

Our annual anthology, *FutureCycle*, combines poetry and flash fiction. The FutureCycle Poetry Book Prize and honorarium is awarded annually for the best full-length volume of poetry we publish in a calendar year. We are dedicated to giving all authors we publish the care their work deserves, making our catalog of titles the most distinguished it can be, and paying forward any earnings to fund more great books.

We've learned a few things about independent publishing over the years. We've also evolved a unique, resilient publishing model that allows us to focus mainly on vetting and preserving for posterity the most books of exceptional quality without becoming overwhelmed with bookkeeping and mailing, fundraising activities, or taxing editorial and production "bubbles." To find out more about what we are doing, come see us at www.futurecycle.org.

www.ingramcontent.com/pod-product-compliance
Lightning Source LLC
Chambersburg PA
CBHW070009100426
42741CB00012B/3168